The Hilarious Dicktionary

Subtle Clues of French Penis Nicknames

THE HILARIOUS DICKTIONARY

SUBTLE CLUES OF FRENCH PENIS NICKNAMES

French saying with a naughty or risqué connotation

LE COUSIN MOELLEUX

GUY BLAISE

*I dedicate this book to lovers everywhere,
paying homage to all men, and offering
a special tribute to the most iconic, enigmatic,
and revered organ of the male body:*

the penis.

Table of Contents

Introduction

"La panne sexuelle, c'est comme une voiture en panne sur l'autoroute de l'amour: ça bloque la circulation." — French saying

(Sexual dysfunction is like a broken-down car on the highway of love: it causes traffic jams.)

Welcome to *The Hilarious French-English Dicktionary: Unveiling the Subtle World of French Penis Nicknames!* Prepare yourself for an amusing journey, as I reveal some of the most amusing French monikers for male members - complete with illustrations and translations! French men display exceptional creativity when it comes to naming their treasured appendages, drawing inspiration from diverse sources, including animal kingdom references, historical figures, biblical quotes, cinematic icons, and even culinary delights!

Penises, often revered and held in high esteem, manifest themselves in various forms: hard or soft, ugly, or beautiful, real, or prosthetic. Across professions and social classes - such as firefighters, mechanics, and vicars – men adore their holy penises! Truly, it's an amazing blessing from above!

But the diversity of penis doesn't end here: be it found among cops, bankers, or politicians Many people enjoy it, which demonstrates its widespread appeal. Who could resist gazing upon the Pope's penis, which may even bear biblical names, like Paul or Moses?

The penis is an endless source of inspiration, reflecting its many facets in French poetry and prose. French men hold this treasured member dearly, and their relationship extends far beyond physical intimacy – it is often expressed through affectionate nicknames.

So, dear reader, with this delightful tome, take some time out for fun and discovery. Play some lively quizzes with your partner or let the language of love take you on a magical voyage - there's nothing like adding an element of playful verbiage into matters of romance!

French culture has an incredible legacy, steeped in romance and cheekiness. Within this rich atmosphere, Frenchmen's penises are held dear as an object of affection and celebration - regardless of size or appearance. This book delves deep into French (unlike most nationalities) male anatomy, exploring its fascinating naming traditions, regardless of taboos!

Within these pages, discover the French language, celebrated for its elegance and finesse. Additionally, ascertain some of the lesser-known biological details about male anatomy, providing insights into essential functions often forgotten. From physiology facts to tales that unravel mysteries surrounding male sexuality - this book promises both education and entertainment - with every page turn!

"Un homme c'est comme une tempête de neige. Tu ne sais pas quand il arrivera, tu ne sais pas combien de centimètres tu auras, et tu ne sais pas combien de temps ça durera." — French saying

(Man is like a snowstorm - you don't know when it will arrive, you don't know how many inches you'll get and you don't know how long it will last.)

L'anguille de caleçon

The underpants eel

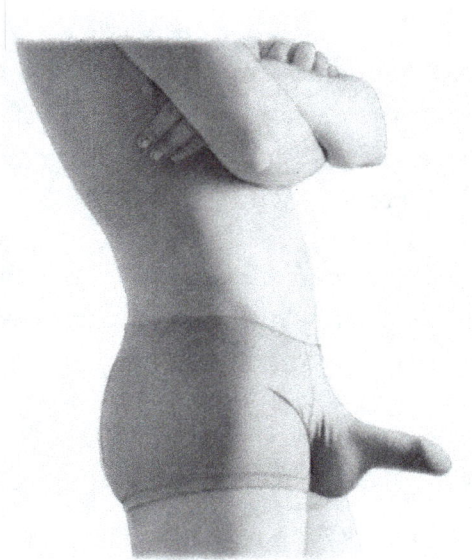

"Une érection, c'est le cadeau que la nature offre à l'homme pour célébrer la vie" — A. Camus

(An erection is the gift that nature offers to a man to celebrate life.)

"Le pénis, c'est comme une baguette: c'est le symbole ultime du charme français!" — Gad Elmaleh

(The penis is like a baguette: it's the ultimate symbol of French charm!)

La baguette   The baguette

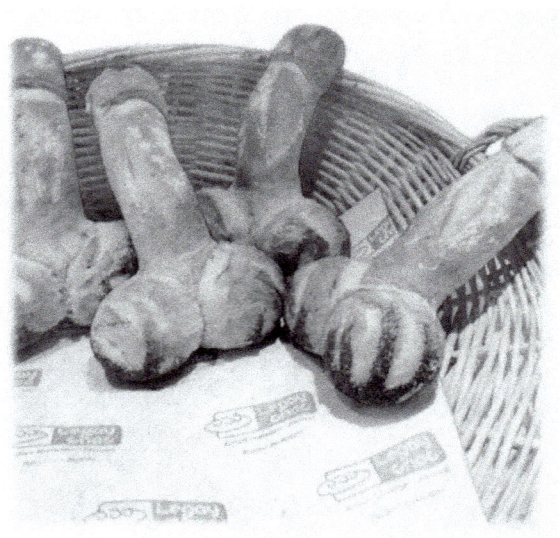

"L'érection, c'est la victoire de l'amour sur la gravité."
— Victor Hugo

(Erection is the victory of love over gravity.)

"Un homme et son pénis sont comme deux musiciens dans un orchestre: parfois en harmonie, mais souvent en désaccord!" — French saying

 (A man and his penis are like two musicians in an orchestra: sometimes in harmony, but often in disagreement!)

Le tire-bouchon   The Corkscrew

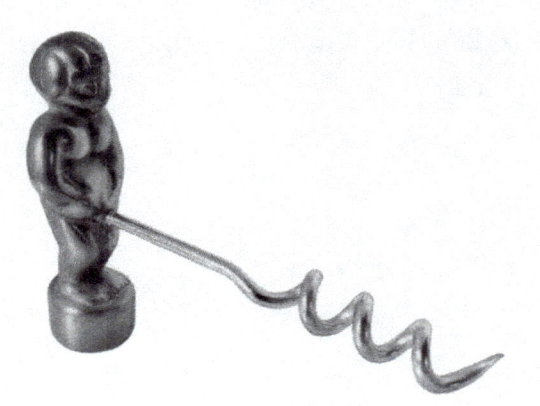

"Faire l'amour, c'est comme jouer une partie d'improvisation, où chaque geste est une réponse à l'autre." — Anne Roumanoff

(Making love is like playing a game of improvisation, where each gesture is a response to the other.)

"Prenez l'habitude de bien baiser votre femme, vous lui éviterez le dérangement d'aller se faire baiser par vos copains." — Frederic Dard

(Get into the habit of fucking your wife well, and you will save her the hassle of having to be fucked by your friends.)

Le zizi rigolo   The funny wiener

"Faire l'amour, c'est comme écrire une comédie romantique, où chaque acte est une blague coquine dans le script de l'amour." — Patrick Bruel

(Making love is like writing a romantic comedy, where each act is a naughty joke in the script of love.)

"L'homme et son pénis: une histoire d'amour sans fin."
— French saying

(A man and his penis: a never-ending love story.)

Le sifflet
enchanté

The enchanted whistle

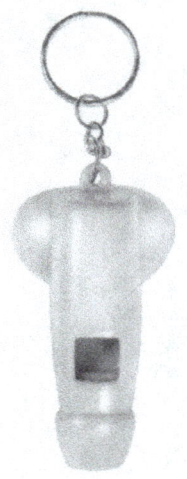

"Un couple n'est vraiment qu'un couple que s'il transpire au lit." — Frederic Dard

(A couple is only a couple if they sweat in bed.)

"La meilleure façon d'aimer quelqu'un, c'est de ne jamais oublier qu'on pourrait le perdre à tout moment."
— Albert Camus

(The best way to love someone is to never forget that you could lose them at any moment.)

Le petit Jules   The little Julius

"Un petit zizi, c'est comme un couteau Suisse: ça ne sert à rien, mais ça peut toujours dépanner." — Coluche

(A small penis is like a Swiss army knife: it's useless, but it can always come in handy.)

"Avoir un petit kiki, c'est comme avoir une petite voiture: ça peut être mignon, mais ça manque de puissance."
— Raymond Devos

(Having a small willy is like having a small car: it can be cute, but it lacks power.)

Le petit Jesus

The little Jesus

"N'avalez rien que Satan essaie de vous enfoncer dans la gorge. Le petit Jésus vient en premier." — GB

(Do not swallow anything Satan is trying to ram down your throat. Little Jesus comes first.)

"Le pénis, c'est comme une montgolfière: ça prend de la hauteur quand ça chauffe en dessous."

— French saying (The penis is like a hot air balloon: it rises when it gets hot below.)

La flute
enchantée

The enchanted flute

"Il vaut mieux être un coquin qu'un hypocrite."
— Coluche

(It's better to be naughty than a hypocrite.)

"Un pénis sans érection, c'est comme une fête sans invités: un peu triste." — French saying

(A penis without an erection is like a party without guests: a bit sad.)

Le serpent malicieux

The mischievous snake

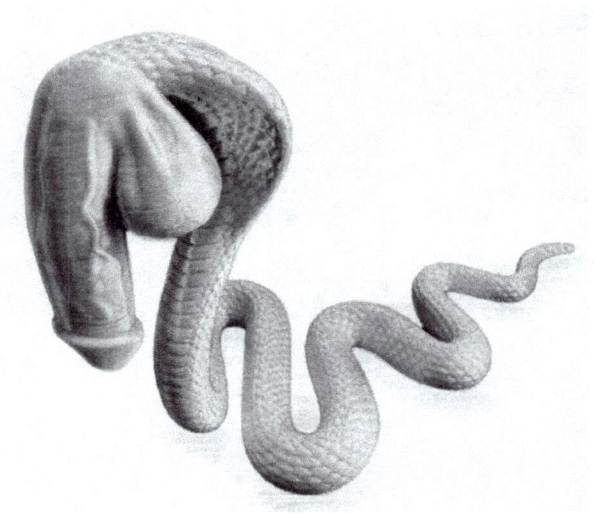

"Le sexe masculin est ce qu'il y a de plus léger au monde, une simple pensée le soulève." — Frederic Dard

(The male sex is the lightest thing in the world: a simple thought lifts it up.)

"L'amour physique, c'est la fusion de deux âmes, dans une danse enflammée où le plaisir est roi." — Muriel Robin

(Physical love is the fusion of two souls in a fiery dance, where pleasure reigns supreme.)

Le petit malin   The little smarty

"Faire l'amour, c'est comme écrire un poème, où chaque mot est une caresse, chaque vers une étreinte."
— Jamel Debbouze

(Making love is like writing a poem, where each word is a caress; each verse an embrace.)

"Aimer, ce n'est pas se regarder l'un l'autre, c'est regarder ensemble dans la même direction."
— Antoine de Saint-Exupéry

(Love is not looking at each other, it is looking together in the same direction.)

Le ministre des
plaisirs

The minister
of pleasures

"Une érection, c'est le tambour battant de la virilité, rythmant la danse envoûtante de l'amour."
— Gad Elmaleh

(An erection is the beating drum of virility, setting the enchanting dance of love in motion.)

"Le pénis, c'est comme une boussole: ça montre toujours le nord." — French saying

(The penis is like a compass: it always points north.)

La banane joyeuse   The happy banana

"Une érection, c'est le rappel à l'ordre de la libido, invitant à la danse des sens." — Anne Roumanoff

(An erection is the reminder of libido, inviting to the dance of the senses.)

"Dans chaque femme, il y a une reine. Parfois, elle a juste besoin de quelqu'un pour la rappeler." — French saying

(In every woman, there is a queen. Sometimes, she just needs someone to remind her.)

La fusée spatiale   The Space Rocket

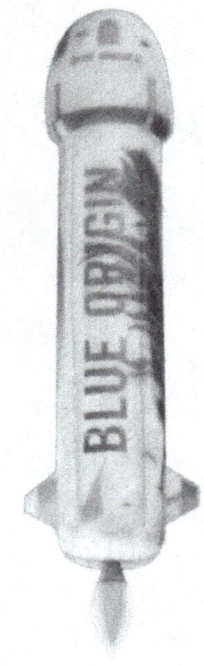

"Faire l'amour, c'est comme composer une symphonie, où chaque mouvement raconte une histoire d'amour infinie."
— Patrick Bruel

(Making love is like composing a symphony, where each movement tells a story of infinite love.)

"Il n'y a pas d'amour sans désir, ni de désir sans amour."
— André Breton

(There is no love without desire, nor desire without love.)

L'hameçon

The hook

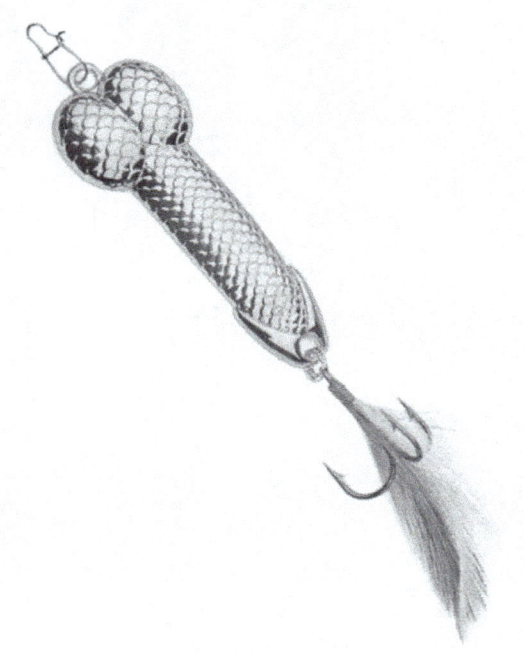

"Le désir sexuel, c'est comme une énigme: parfois difficile à comprendre, mais toujours captivant." — Lucien

(Sexual desire is like a puzzle: sometimes hard to understand, but always captivating.)

"Aimer, ce n'est pas se regarder l'un l'autre, c'est regarder ensemble dans la même direction."
— Antoine de Saint-Exupéry

(Love is not looking at each other - it is looking together in the same direction.)

Le ramoneur   The chimney sweep

"L'amour, c'est l'alchimie mystérieuse de deux corps, se fondant l'un dans l'autre dans un tourbillon de sensations." — Florence Foresti

(Love is the mysterious alchemy of two bodies, melting into each other in a whirlwind of sensations.)

"On ne voit bien qu'avec le cœur. L'essentiel est invisible pour les yeux." — Antoine de Saint-Exupéry

(One sees clearly only with the heart. The essential is invisible to the eyes.)

Le bâton qui rend fou

The stick that
drives you crazy

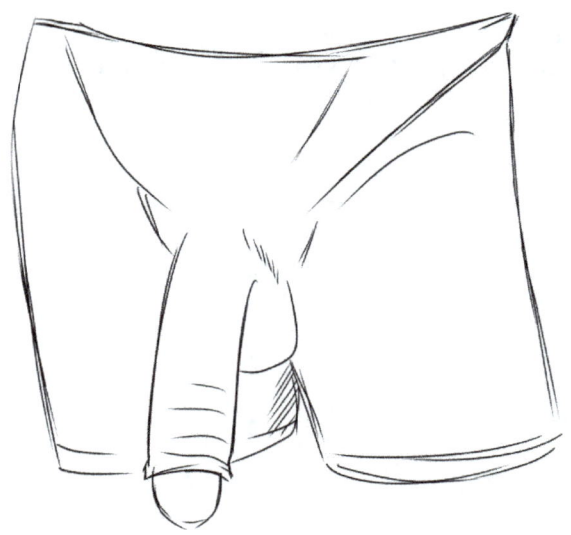

"Une érection, c'est le sursaut de la pulsion, propulsant l'homme vers les cimes de l'extase." — Florence Foresti

(An erection is the surge of impulse, propelling man towards the heights of ecstasy.)

"Un pénis sans érection, c'est comme un téléphone sans batterie: ça ne sert à rien." — GB

(A penis without an erection is like a phone without a battery: it's useless.)

Service-trois-pieces   Three-piece service

"Le mariage est comme un bon repas: à chaque fois que vous le réchauffez, il devient de nouveau délicieux."
— French Saying

(Marriage is like a good meal: every time you warm it up, it becomes delicious again.)

"L'amour est comme une rose: chaque pétale est une illusion, chaque épine une réalité." — Alfred de Musset

(Love is like a rose: each petal is an illusion; each thorn, a reality.)

Le dard

The stinger

"Un mariage réussi repose sur l'art de dire 'oui cherie' au bon moment." — French saying

(A successful marriage relies on the art of saying "yes, dear" at the right moment.)

"Il n'y a qu'un seul bonheur dans la vie, c'est d'aimer et d'être aimé." — George Sand

(There is only one happiness in life: to love and be loved.)

Le cigare a moustache   The moustache cigar

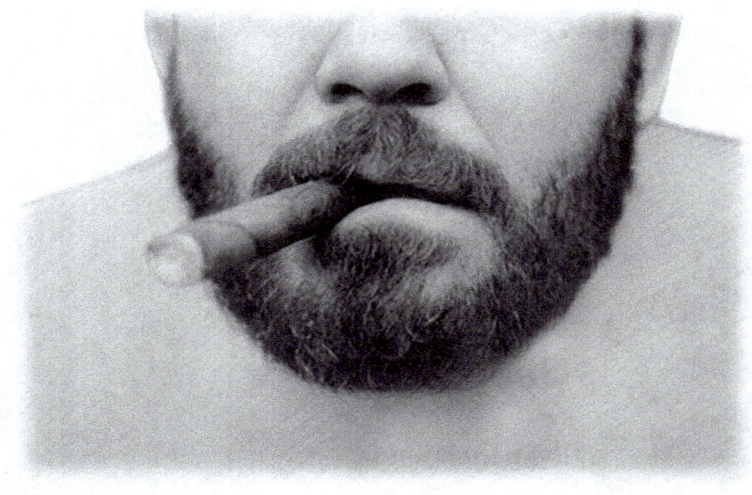

"Le secret d'un mariage heureux réside dans la capacité à entendre 'je t'aime' même lorsque le partenaire ronfle."
— French saying

(The secret to a happy marriage lies in the ability to hear "I love you" even when your partner is snoring.)

"Faire l'amour, c'est comme faire la cuisine. Il faut savoir doser les ingrédients pour que le plat soit réussi."
— Elie Kakou

(Making love is like cooking You must know how to balance the ingredients for the dish to be successful.)

La bistouquette

Wang

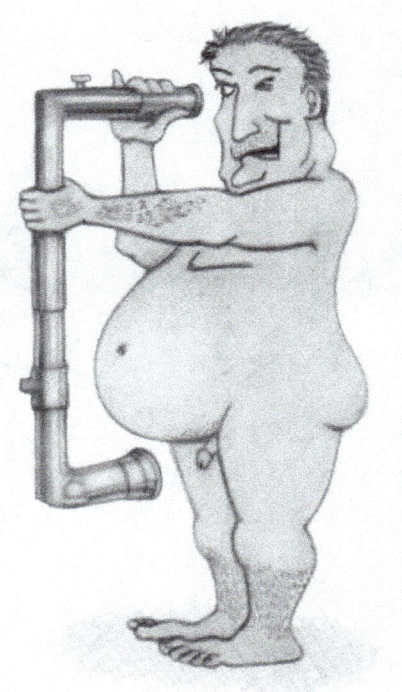

"La panne sexuelle, c'est comme un feu d'artifice mouillé:
ça fait beaucoup de bruit, mais ça n'explose jamais."
— French saying

(Sexual dysfunction is like a damp firework: it makes a
lot of noise, but it never goes off.)

"Le sexe, c'est le ciment du couple. Sans ça, ça s'effrite."
— Jean-Marie Bigard

(Sex is the cement of a couple - without it, everything
falls apart.)

La quequette   Willy

"La panne sexuelle, c'est comme une mauvaise connexion internet: ça coupe au moment crucial." — GB

(Sexual dysfunction is like a bad internet connection: it cuts out at the crucial moment.)

"L'amour, c'est comme le café. Ça réchauffe le cœur et ça donne de l'énergie." — Laurent Baffie

(Love is like coffee. It warms the heart and gives you energy.)

La zigounette

Dick

"La panne sexuelle, c'est comme un téléphone sans batterie: ça rend les échanges difficiles." — GB

(Sexual dysfunction is like a phone with no battery: it makes communication difficult.)

"Le sexe, c'est comme une bonne blague. Ça fait rire et ça met de bonne humeur." — Muriel Robin

(Sex is like a good joke. It makes you laugh and puts you in a good mood.)

La biroute The windsock

"La taille du pénis est comme le poids d'un livre - il ne dit rien sur son contenu." — GB

(Penis size is like the weight of a book – it says nothing about its contents.)

"Le sexe, c'est comme une partie de football. Il faut marquer des buts pour gagner." — Francky Vincent

(Sex is like a game of football. You must score goals to win.)

President Mao   Chairman Mao

"La taille du pénis importe peu, c'est la façon dont on s'en sert qui compte." — GB

(Penis size doesn't matter much, it's how you use it that counts.)

"Un pénis sans érection, c'est comme un ballon dégonflé: ça manque de gonflant."

(A penis without an erection is like a deflated balloon: it lacks puffiness.)

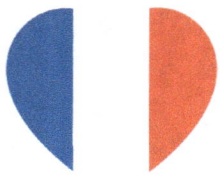

Le Cubain   The Cuban

"Dans le lit, les secrets se révèlent et les désirs s'épanouissent." — French saying

(In bed, secrets are revealed and desires flourish.)

"Le pénis est le chef-d'œuvre de l'amour, sculpté avec soin par la main de la nature." — V. Hugo

(The penis is the masterpiece of love, carefully sculpted by the hand of nature.)

Le noeud   The knot

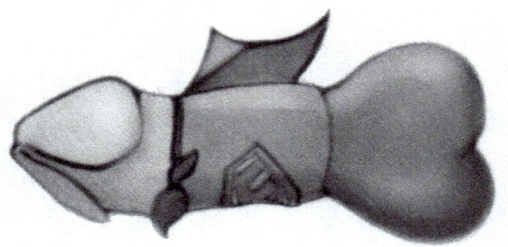

"Les couilles, c'est comme des pommes de terre dans un sac: elles roulent toujours vers le bas!" — French saying

(Balls are like potatoes in a sack: they always roll downwards.)

"La virilité ne se mesure pas à la taille de l'outil, mais à l'intensité du feu qui l'anime." — A. France

(Virility is not measured by the size of the tool, but by the intensity of the fire that animates it.)

La bite   The cock

"Avoir une grosse bite, c'est comme être une rock star: ça rend les fans hystériques!" — French saying

(Having a big dick is like being a rock star: it drives fans crazy!)

"La véritable grandeur d'un homme ne se mesure pas à la taille de son pénis, mais à la force de son caractère."
— Victor Hugo

(The true greatness of a man is not measured by the size of his penis, but by the strength of his character.)

La queue   **The tail**

"Avoir une grosse bite, c'est comme avoir un super-pouvoir: ça donne l'impression d'être invincible!" — GB

(Having a big dick is like having a superpower: it makes you feel invincible!)

"La taille importe peu, c'est la manière dont vous l'utilisez." — GB

(Size matters little; it's how you use it.)

Popaul   Paul

"Un homme avec un grand ego et une petite bite, c'est comme un lion en peluche: ça rugit mais ça ne fait pas peur!" — French saying

(A man with a big ego and a small dick is like a plush lion: it roars but it doesn't scare anyone!)

"Le pénis: un outil livré sans mode d'emploi, et pourtant tout homme se prend pour un maître en mécanique."
— Blaise

(The penis: a tool that comes with no instruction manual, yet every man thinks he's a master mechanic.)

La banane   Banana

"L'ego d'un homme peut être aussi fragile que sa bite: il suffit d'un petit coup pour le faire tomber!" — GB

(A man's ego can be as fragile as his dick: it only takes a little knock to bring it down!)

"L'ego d'un homme est comme son pénis: plus, il grossit, plus il est difficile à gérer." — GB

(A man's ego is like his penis: the bigger it gets, the harder it is to handle.)

Le champion   The champion

Un homme avec un ego surdimensionné et une petite bite, c'est comme un ballon gonflé à l'hélium: beaucoup de bruit pour pas grand chose!" — GB

(A man with an oversized ego and a small dick is like a balloon inflated with helium: lots of noise for nothing much!)

"L'amour, c'est comme une fête. Il faut savoir s'amuser et profiter de chaque instant." — Anne Roumanoff

(Love is like a party. You must know how to have fun and enjoy every moment.)

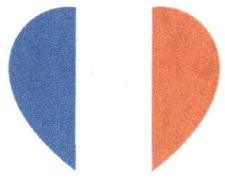

Lui   Him

"L'ego d'un homme est comme sa bite: il est toujours plus gros dans sa tête!" — French saying

(A man's ego is like his dick: it's always bigger in his head!)

"Un penis gallant est celui qui se leve pour laisser un femme s'assoir." — GB

(A gallant penis is one who stands up to let a woman sit down.)

Le gourdin   The club

"L'esprit d'un homme est comme sa bite: il peut être intelligent, mais il peut aussi être complètement déconnecté!" — GB

(A man's mind is like his dick: it can be intelligent, but it can also be completely disconnected!)

"On dit que la taille ne compte pas, mais franchement, qui voudrait d'une baguette toute molle?"
— Florence Foresti

(They say size doesn't matter, but honestly, who would want a limp baguette?)

Le joystick

The joystick

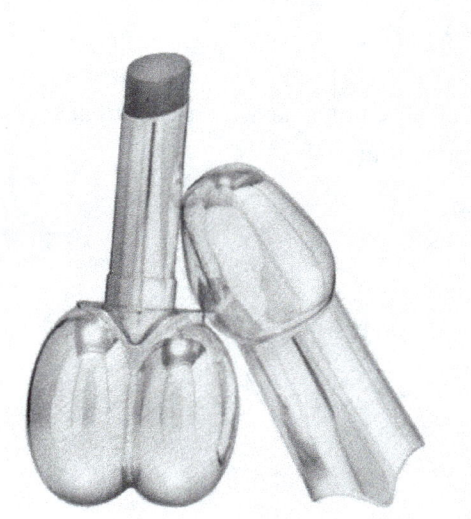

"Un homme sans pénis est comme un oiseau sans ailes."
— GB

(A man without a penis is like a bird without wings.)

"Le pénis est comme un-GPS: parfois il vous conduit sur une mauvaise route, mais vous arrivez quand même à destination." — Elizabeth T.

(The penis is like a GPS: sometimes it leads you down the wrong road, but you still arrive at your destination.)

L'asperge

Asparagus

"Un bon amant, c'est comme un bon vin: il s'améliore
avec le temps et laisse un goût délicieux en bouche."
— French saying

(A good lover is like a good wine: he gets better with time
and leaves a delightful taste in your mouth.)

"Un pénis sans érection, c'est comme un avion sans
carburant: ça ne décolle pas." — GB

(A penis without an erection is like a plane without fuel:
it doesn't take off.)

Le missile de l'amour   The love missile

"Un bon amant, c'est celui qui te fait sentir comme la seule femme au monde, même lorsque vous êtes entourés par la foule." — French saying

(A good lover is someone who makes you feel like the only woman in the world, even when you're surrounded by a crowd.)

"Le pénis, c'est comme un crayon: plus, il est taillé, mieux il écrit." — Laurent Baffie

(The penis is like a pencil: the more sharpened it is, the better it writes.)

Terminateur

Terminator

"La performance au lit, c'est un peu comme un spectacle: il faut donner le meilleur de soi-même pour faire vibrer le public!" — Jamel Debbouze

(Performance in bed is a bit like a show: you must give your best to thrill the audience!)

"Le pénis: la seule chose dans la vie qui peut être à la fois une bénédiction et une malédiction, souvent en même temps." — GB

(The penis: the only thing in life that can be both a blessing and a curse, often at the same time.)

Le Gladiateur

The Gladiator

"La libido, c'est comme une météo capricieuse: on ne sait jamais quand le soleil reviendra briller!" — Éric et Ramzy

(The libido is like unpredictable weather: you never know when the sun will come back to shine!)

"Le pénis est comme une carte de credit: c'est amusant de l'avoir jusqu'à ce que vous l'ayez atteint au maximum et que vous ne puissiez plus effectuer le paiement minimum." — J. Maurice

(The penis is like a credit card: it's fun to have until you max it out and can't make the minimum payment.)

Godzilla · Godzilla

"Faire l'amour, c'est comme jouer au poker: parfois, tu bluffes et ça marche. Mais d'autres fois, tu te retrouves avec une main pourrie!" — Anne Roumanoff

(Making love is like playing poker: sometimes, you bluff, and it works. But other times, you end up with a lousy hand!)

"Le pénis, c'est comme un volcan: il peut entrer en éruption à tout moment!" — Anne Roumanoff

(The penis is like a volcano: it can erupt at any moment!)

Le General

The General

"L'érection, ce murmure du désir qui se transforme en cri de plaisir." — Antoine T.

(Erection, this whisper of desire that turns into a cry of pleasure.)

"Le pénis, c'est comme un marteau: il peut construire ou démolir, selon comment on s'en sert."
— Valérie Lemercier

(The penis is like a hammer: it can build or demolish, depending on how it's used.)

Le Pistolet

The pistol

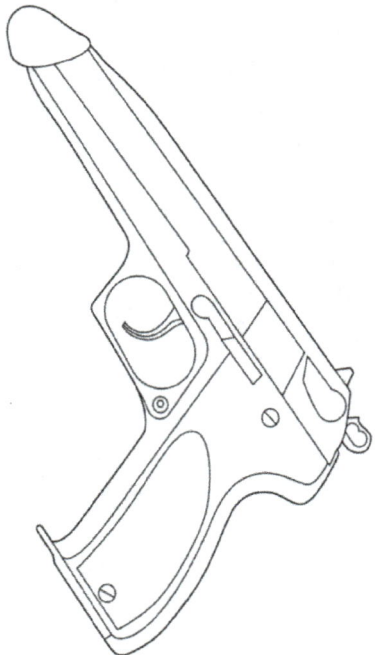

"L'érection, c'est le réveil en fanfare de la virilité endormie." — Stéphane Guillo

(The erection is the wake-up call of slumbering virility.)

"La masturbation, c'est comme une séance de cinéma en solo: vous êtes à la fois le spectateur et la star."— Paul

(Masturbation is like a solo movie session: you're both the audience and the star.)

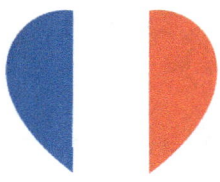

Le bâton   The stick

"Un bon mari, c'est celui qui te fait sentir en sécurité dans ses bras, et t'accompagne dans tous les défis de la vie avec courage et dévouement." — French saying

(A good husband is someone who makes you feel safe in his arms and accompanies you in all the challenges of life with courage and dedication.)

"On dit que le pénis est l'organe de l'homme, mais parfois, c'est lui qui nous contrôle!" — Jamel Debbouze

(They say the penis is the man's organ, but sometimes, it's the one controlling us!)

Les bijoux de famille   The family jewlery

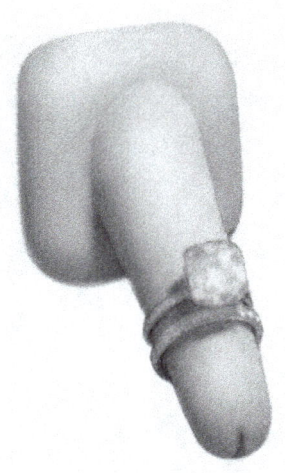

"Un bon amant, c'est celui qui embrase ton corps autant que ton esprit, laissant une empreinte indélébile sur ton âme." — French saying

(A good lover is someone who ignites your body as much as your mind, leaving an indelible mark on your soul.)

"Un pénis, c'est comme une antenne: il capte les ondes de plaisir!" — Laurent Baffie

(A penis is like an antenna: it picks up waves of pleasure!)

Charles le chauve

Charles the Bald

"Une érection, c'est le sursaut de la pulsion, propulsant l'homme vers les cimes de l'extase." — Florence Foresti

(An erection is the surge of impulse, propelling man towards the heights of ecstasy.)

"Le pénis, c'est comme un couteau Suisse: il a plusieurs fonctions, mais attention aux accidents!" — Elie Semoun

(The penis is like a Swiss army knife: it has multiple functions...but watch out for accidents!)

La nouille   The noodle

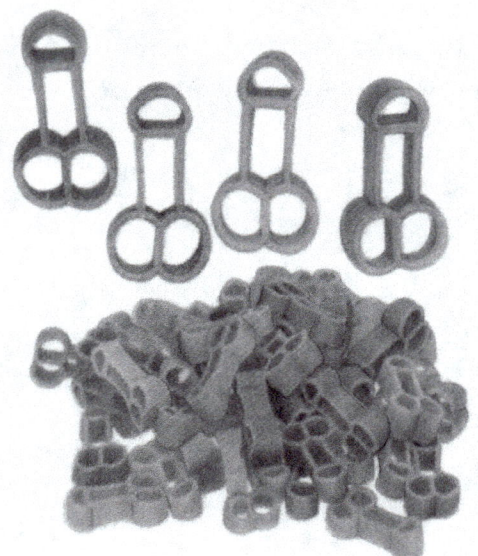

"La masturbation, c'est comme une séance de bricolage:
tu utilises tes outils pour construire ton propre plaisir."
— Laurent Baffie

(Masturbation is like a DIY session: you use your tools to
build your own pleasure.)

"La libido, c'est comme une baguette magique: parfois,
elle prend des vacances sans préavis!" — Gad Elmaleh

(Libido is like a magic wand: sometimes, it takes
unexpected holidays!)

Le bazooka   The bazooka

"La masturbation, c'est comme une session de spa pour ton cerveau: ça détend et ça libère les endorphines."
— Anne Roumanoff

(Masturbation is like a spa session for your brain: it relaxes and releases endorphins.)

"Quand la libido décide de faire grève, même la plus belle des femmes ne peut la convaincre de revenir au travail!"
— Florence Foresti

(When libido decides to go on strike, not even the most beautiful woman can convince it to come back to work!)

Le revolver   The revolver

"La masturbation, c'est l'art de se faire des câlins tout seul." — Laurent Baffie

(Masturbation is the art of giving yourself cuddles all alone.)

"L'abstinence est la meilleure garantie contre les maladies sexuellement transmissibles." — Jules Ferre

(Abstinence is the best guarantee against sexually transmitted diseases.)

La Grosse Bertha

Big Bertha

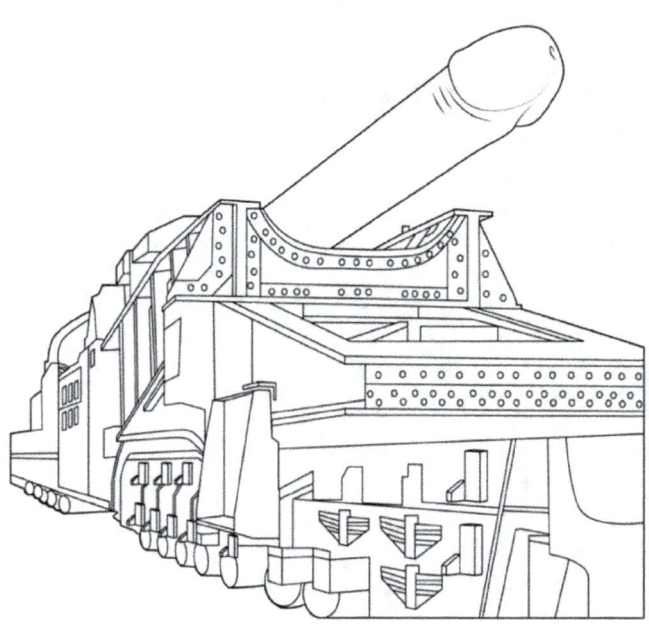

"La masturbation, c'est comme un voyage en solitaire: tu explores les territoires inconnus de ton corps et tu découvres des trésors cachés." — Gad Elmaleh

(Masturbation is like a solo journey: you explore the unknown territories of your body and discover hidden treasures.)

"Le sexe, c'est comme la cuisine: ça demande de la technique, de la passion et parfois quelques brûlures." — Frederic Dard.

(Sex is like cooking - it requires technique, passion and, sometimes, a few burns."

Le tuyau

The pipe

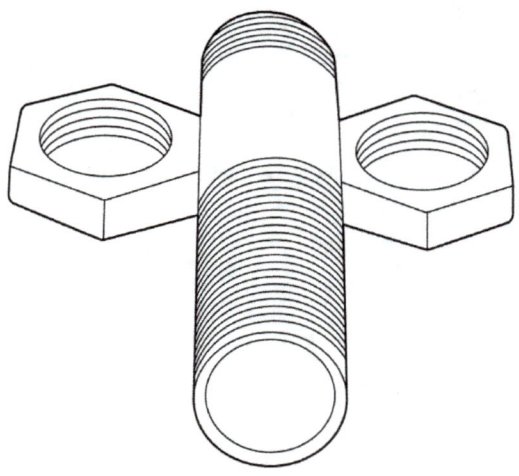

"Être accro au sexe, c'est comme être pris dans un tourbillon: tu tournes en rond sans jamais trouver la sortie." — Florence Foresti

(Being addicted to sex is like being caught in a whirlwind: you go around in circles and never find the way out.)

"La libido, c'est comme une batterie: quand elle est à plat, plus rien ne peut la recharger!" — Anne Roumanoff

(Libido is like a battery: when it's flat, nothing can recharge it!)

La mèche

The wick

"Le sexe masculin est ce qu'il y a de plus léger au monde, une simple pensée le soulève." — F. Dard

(The male sex is the lightest thing in the world - a simple thought lifts it.)

"Le sexe, c'est comme le WIFI: quand ça marche, ça te facilite la vie. Mais quand ça bug, ça te fout en rogne!" — Florence Foresti

(Sex is like wifi: when it works, it makes your life easier. But when it glitches, it makes you angry!)

Le singe   The monkey

"Faites l'amour, pas la guerre. Ou alors faites les deux: mariez-vous." — French saying

(Make love, not war. Or do both: get married.)

"La fellation, c'est l'expression ultime de l'amour et de la complicité entre amants, un geste de tendresse et de passion." — GB

(A blow job is the ultimate expression of love and complicity between lovers, a gesture of tenderness and passion.)

Sucette a la viande   Meat lollipop

"Que feraient les hommes sans les femmes? La lessive et la vaisselle." — French joke

(What would men do without women? Laundry and dishes.)

"Faire l'amour, c'est comme cuisiner: ça peut être délicieux ou ça peut être un vrai fiasco!" — Jamel Debbouze

(Making love is like cooking: it can be delicious, or it can be a total disaster!)

L'affolant   The maddening

"Quand la libido fait la grasse matinée, même le café le plus fort ne peut la réveiller!" — Claudia Tagbo

(When libido sleeps in, not even the strongest coffee can wake it up!)

"Quand le sexe est mauvais, même la météo semble plus intéressante!" — Florence Foresti

(When sex is bad, even the weather seems more interesting!)

Le Bâton de chair · The staff of flesh

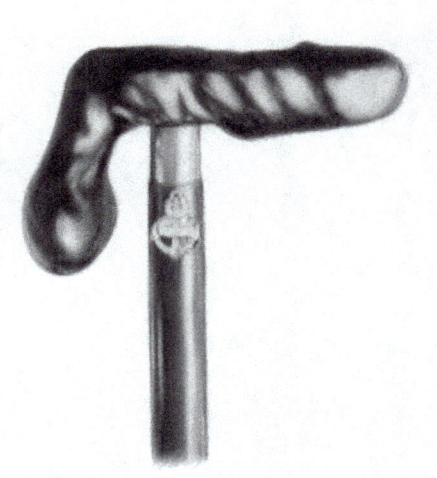

"L'appétit sexuel, c'est le phare qui guide nos étreintes passionnées." — French saying

(Sexual appetite is the lighthouse that guides our passionate embraces.)

"L'orgasme, c'est le miracle qui transforme un simple instant en une éternité de félicité, où le corps et l'âme fusionnent dans une extase divine." — GB

(Orgasm is the miracle that transforms a simple moment into an eternity of bliss, where body and soul merge in divine ecstasy.)

Le baton de Moise   The staff of Moses

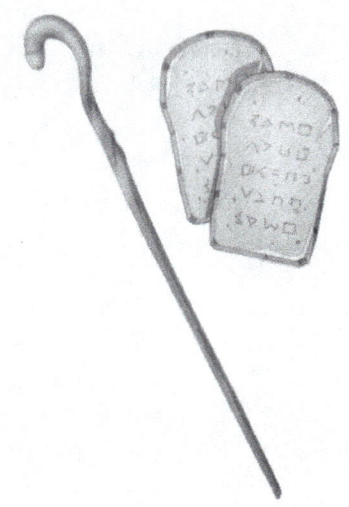

"La libido, c'est comme une bougie: parfois, elle s'éteint sans crier gare!" — Franck Dubosc

(Libido is like a candle: sometimes, it goes out without warning!)

"La masturbation, c'est le seul sport où tu es à la fois l'entraîneur, l'arbitre et le champion." — Kyan Khojandi

(Masturbation is the only sport where, at the same time, you're the coach, the referee, and the champion.)

Le petit diable

The little devil

"Dans la symphonie de l'amour, l'orgasme est la note finale, celle qui résonne encore longtemps après la fin du concert." — GB

(In the symphony of love, orgasm is the final note; the one that still resonates long after the concert has ended.)

"La masturbation, c'est le rituel du soir pour les célibataires: un peu comme une prière avant de dormir." — Anne Roumanoff

(Masturbation is the evening ritual for singles: a bit like a prayer before bedtime.)

Le pivot de la joie   The pivot of joy

"Un mauvais coup, c'est comme lire un mauvais livre: tu te demandes pourquoi tu as perdu ton temps et tu veux jeter le livre par la fenêtre." — GB

(Bad sex is like reading a bad book: you wonder why you wasted your time, and you want to throw the book out the window.)

"L'amour, c'est le soleil qui réchauffe nos cœurs et illumine nos vies, rendant chaque journée un peu plus belle que la précédente." — GB

(Love is the sun that warms our hearts and illuminates our lives, making each day a little more beautiful than the last.)

Le flambeau de
l'amour

The torch of love

"L'appétit sexuel, c'est le jardin secret de nos fantasmes."

(Sexual appetite is the secret garden of our fantasies.)

"La masturbation, c'est l'art de se faire des câlins tout seul." — Laurent Baffie

(Masturbation is the art of giving yourself cuddles all alone.)

Le monstre   The monster

"L'appétit sexuel est le carburant de la vie amoureuse."
— French saying.

(Sexual appetite is the fuel of love life.)

"Le sexe sans amour c'est comme une journée sans soleil."
— Pierre D.

(Sex without love is like a day without sunshine.)

L'Anaconda   Anaconda

"Un mari jaloux est comme un détective privé: il passe son temps à chercher des indices, mais il oublie qu'il est le seul à créer son propre drame." — Antoine

(A jealous husband is like a private detective: he spends his time searching for clues, but he forgets that he's the one creating his own drama.)

"Lorsqu'un homme parle de sa bite, c'est souvent son cerveau qui parle à sa place!" — GB

(When a man talks about his dick, it's often his brain speaking.)

Le cerveau du Monsieur   The husband's brain

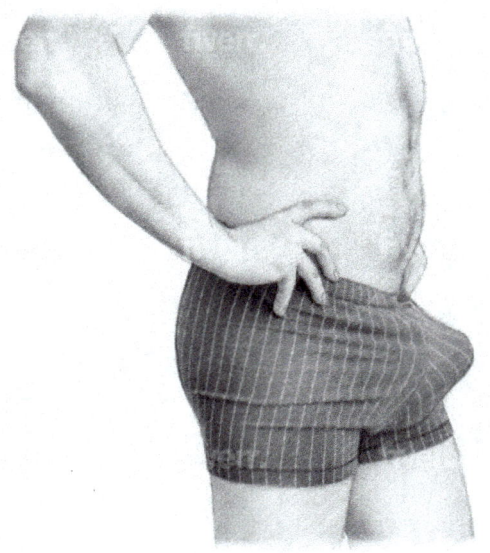

"Pourquoi certains hommes donnent-ils un prénom à leur penis? Ils veulent être plus intimes avec celui qui prend toutes les décisions pour eux!" — French joke

(Why do some men give their penis a name? They want to be more intimate with the one who makes all the decisions for them!)

"Le pénis, c'est comme une pièce de monnaie: il a deux côtés, mais c'est toujours la même valeur!" — Jamel Debbouze

(The penis is like a coin: it has two sides, but it's always the same value!)

L'andouillette

Sausage

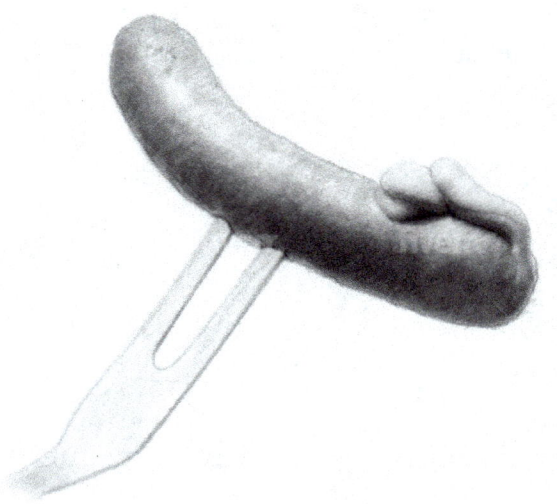

"Le désir sexuel, c'est comme une braise: il suffit d'un souffle pour le raviver." — Olivier

(Sexual desire is like an ember: it only takes a breath to rekindle it.)

"Le pénis, c'est comme une clé USB: il peut stocker des souvenirs inoubliables!" — Valérie Lemercier

(The penis is like a USB key: it can store unforgettable memories!)

L'aubergine   Eggplant

"L'homme infidèle, c'est comme un miroir brisé: il ne reflète que des fragments de fidélité." — Frederic

(The unfaithful man is like a broken mirror: he only reflects fragments of fidelity.)

"On dit que le pénis est l'arme secrète de l'homme, mais parfois, c'est lui qui se tire dessus!" — Laurent Gerra

(They say the penis is the man's secret weapon, but, sometimes, it's the one shooting itself!)

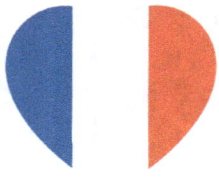

Superman   Superman

"L'homme infidèle, c'est comme une page blanche: il écrit son histoire sentimentale avec des mots volés." — Nancy

(The unfaithful man is like a blank page: he writes his romantic story with stolen words.)

"Un pénis, c'est comme une bougie: il peut illuminer les nuits les plus sombres!" — Elie Semoun

(A penis is like a candle: it can light up the darkest nights!)

Le petit frere   The little brother

"L'homme infidèle, c'est comme un acteur de théâtre: il joue plusieurs rôles dans différentes pièces."
— French saying

(The unfaithful man is like a theater actor: he plays multiple roles in different plays.)

"Le pénis, c'est comme une comédie: il peut faire rire et pleurer en même temps!"— Gad Elmaleh

(The penis is like a comedy: it can make you laugh and cry at the same time!)

La jambe du milieu   The middle leg

"L'homme infidèle, c'est comme un oiseau migrateur: il vole de nid en nid sans jamais se poser." — French saying.

(The unfaithful man is like a migratory bird: he flies from nest to nest without ever settling down.)

"Un pénis, c'est comme une baguette de pain: il faut le pétrir avec amour pour qu'il soit bien cuit!"
— Anne Roumanoff

(A penis is like a loaf of bread: it needs to be kneaded with love to be well-baked!)

Le petit soldat
qui se met au
garde a vous

The little soldier
standing at attention.

"La sexualité, c'est un langage universel qui transcende les barrières culturelles." — French saying

(Sexuality is a universal language that transcends cultural barriers.)

French Heat:
20 Naughty Phrases for
Intimate Moments

Être performant au lit, c'est comme être un artiste: il faut captiver son audience jusqu'au dernier acte! — Gad Elmaleh: Being good in bed is like being an artist: you must captivate your audience until the last act.

Je veux te goûter jusqu'au dernier souffle: "I want to taste you until the last breath."

Je veux te sentir contre moi: "I want to feel you against me." Expresses a desire for physical closeness and intimacy.

Tu me rends fou/folle: "You drive me crazy." Conveys intense desire and arousal.

J'ai envie de toi: "I want you." Expresses sexual desire and attraction.

Tu es tellement sexy: "You are so sexy." Heightens arousal and boosts confidence.

Embrasse-moi: "Kiss me." Sets the mood for intimacy and passion.

Je vais te faire plaisir: "I'm going to please you." Promises sexual satisfaction and is highly arousing.

Viens plus près: "Come closer." Creates a sense of anticipation and intimacy.

Je veux te goûter: "I want to taste you." Expresses a desire for oral pleasure.

Plus fort: "Harder." Intensifies pleasure and arousal.

Je veux te faire l'amour: "I want to make love to you." Conveys deep emotional and physical connection.

J'aime quand tu me prends sauvagement: "I love it when you take me passionately."

Tu me fais mouiller tellement fort: "You make me so wet."

Je veux sentir tout ton corps contre le mien: "I want to feel your entire body against mine."

Fais-moi jouir encore et encore: "Make me come again and again."

Je te veux en moi maintenant: "I want you inside me now."

Tes mains me rendent folle de désir: "Your hands drive me crazy with desire."

Je suis à toi, prends-moi comme tu veux: "I'm yours, take me as you want."

Mords-moi, je veux sentir ta passion: "Bite me, I want to feel your passion."

Baise-moi comme jamais auparavant: "Fuck me like never before."

Know Your Partner:
20 Questions to Test Your
Relationship IQ

"Un bon amant, c'est celui qui sait lire entre les lignes de ton corps et composer la symphonie de ton plaisir."
— French saying

*(A good lover is someone who knows how to read
between the lines of your body and compose
the symphony of your pleasure.)*

Navigating romantic relationships can be likened to paddling a long river and encountering various weather conditions along the way. To assist on this voyage, here's a roadmap designed to help you better understand your partner and earn his/her affection. Answer 20 questions, with an average score of 80% or above, to gauge how skilled of a lover you are. This game provides a fun, yet straight-forward, approach towards deepening the connection with your partner; men who understand their partners tend to find greater satisfaction in bed!

Does he/she prefer:

Sucré ou salé? EMPTY BOX FOR ANSWERS BETWEEN ENGLISH-FRENCH (Sweet or salty?)

Chiens ou chats? (Dogs or cats?)

Été ou hiver? (Summer or winter?)

Café ou thé? (Coffee or tea?)

Vie en ville ou à la campagne? (City life or Country life?)

_____

Plage ou montagne? (Beach or mountain getaway?)

_____

Lève-tôt ou oiseau de nuit? (Early riser or night owl?)

_____

Introverti ou extraverti? (Introvert or extrovert?)

_____

Livres ou films? (Books or films?)

_____

Télé-réalité ou documentaires? (Reality TV or documentaries?)

_____

Manger au restaurant ou cuisiner à la maison? (Eat out or cook at home?)

_____

Comédie ou drame? (Comedy or drama?)

_____

Argent ou renommée? (Money or fame?)

_____

Voyager seul ou avec des amis? (Travel alone or with friends?)

_____

Aventure ou détente? (Adventure or relaxation?)

_____

Spontanéité ou planification detaillee? (Spontaneity or careful planning?)

_____

Livres physiques ou e-books? (Physical books or e-books?)

_____

Rester à la maison ou sortir vendredi soir? (Home or out Friday night?)

_____

Rock classique ou pop moderne? (Classic rock or modern pop?)

_____

Temps ensemble ou espace personnel? (Time together or space apart?

_____

Saucy French:
A Playful Exploration
of Naughty French Expressions

"La coquinerie, c'est le petit grain de folie qui pimente la vie."
— French quote

(Naughtiness is the little touch of madness that spices up life.)

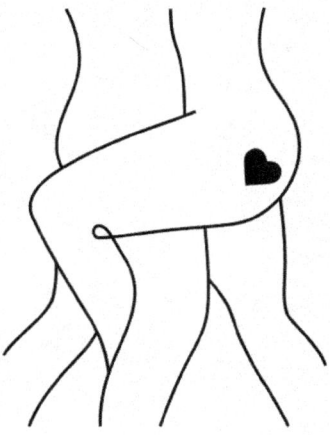

If you studied French in college, chances are you probably didn't come across any of these fun French phrases in class. Don't despair - adding something interesting and unexpected to your linguistic repertoire never goes out of style!

Navigating the complex nuances of love and intimacy can be tricky, but French provides an abundance of euphemisms and metaphors that provide romantic yet colorful language for those wanting to add some spark into their conversations.

Given the rich vocabulary in French, particularly regarding human anatomy and sexuality, it's understandable that some may mistake this linguistic richness for obsession. Although French speakers do tend towards elegance in speech patterns and expression, they're not afraid to add playful terms, like "cul" (ass), into their conversations.

So, now it's time to add some French flavor into your vocabulary! Sit back, unwind, and take pleasure in this amusing selection of French naughty metaphors and euphemisms related to love making (faire l'amour) - flirtatious expressions that have been specially chosen for you!

La partie de jambes en l'air: The game of legs in the air. This metaphor humorously describes lovemaking as a playful and energetic activity, emphasizing the act's physicality.

La gymnastique horizontale: Horizontal gymnastics. This metaphor playfully compares lovemaking to a gymnastics routine, highlighting the flexibility and agility required for satisfying sexual encounters.

La partie de cache-cache sous la couette: The game of hide-and-seek under the covers. This metaphor adds a playful and clandestine element to lovemaking, suggesting a sense of spontaneity and excitement.

La chasse au trésor sous les draps: The treasure hunt under the sheets. This metaphor humorously describes lovemaking as an adventurous quest for pleasure and satisfaction.

La partie de cache-cache à la chandelle: The game of hide-and-seek by candlelight. This metaphor adds a romantic and clandestine element to lovemaking, suggesting a sense of mystery and intimacy.

Le marathon des câlins: The cuddle marathon. This metaphor humorously portrays lovemaking as a long and enjoyable journey of physical affection and intimacy.

Le concours de la position la plus bizarre: The contest for the most bizarre position. This metaphor adds a humorous and adventurous element to lovemaking, suggesting a playful exploration of different positions and techniques.

La symphonie des soupirs et des gémissements: The symphony of sighs and moans. This metaphor humorously portrays lovemaking as a melodious and passionate exchange of vocal expressions of pleasure.

La réunion des corps en folie: The gathering of bodies in frenzy. This metaphor adds a wild and uninhibited element to lovemaking, suggesting a sense of abandon and ecstasy.

La course à l'orgasme: The race to orgasm. This metaphor humorously describes lovemaking as a competitive pursuit, highlighting the intensity and urgency of sexual pleasure.

Le tour de magie sous les draps: The magic trick under the sheets. This metaphor playfully suggests that lovemaking can be a mysterious and enchanting experience, full of surprises and delights.

La séance d'entraînement pour les abdos: The abs work-out session. This metaphor humorously portrays lovemaking as a physical activity that can provide a workout for the abdominal muscles, adding a playful twist to the experience.

Le défilé des postures acrobatiques: The parade of acrobatic positions. This metaphor adds a playful and adventurous element to lovemaking, suggesting a creative exploration of different sexual positions.

La dégustation de plaisirs sucrés: The tasting of sweet pleasures. This metaphor humorously portrays lovemaking as a sensory experience akin to savoring delicious treats, highlighting the indulgence and enjoyment of the moment.

La séance de bricolage intime: The intimate DIY session. This metaphor humorously suggests that lovemaking involves a hands-on approach to pleasure and satisfaction, likening it to a DIY project.

La danse endiablée des draps: The frenzied dance of the sheets. This metaphor adds a lively and energetic element to lovemaking, evoking imagery of passionate movements and entanglements.

La course-poursuite érotique: The erotic chase. This metaphor humorously portrays lovemaking as a playful pursuit of pleasure and excitement, suggesting a sense of anticipation and thrill.

Le rodéo des plaisirs charnels: The rodeo of carnal pleasures. This metaphor adds a playful and adventurous element to lovemaking, suggesting a wild and untamed ride of sensual delights.

La symphonie des caresses: The symphony of caresses. This metaphor portrays lovemaking as a harmonious and melodious exchange of sensual touches and gestures, evoking a sense of intimacy and connection.

La séance de dégustation des fruits défendus: The tasting of forbidden fruit. This metaphor humorously suggests that lovemaking involves indulging in forbidden pleasures and desires, adding a playful and mischievous twist to the experience.

Le tourbillon des émotions: The whirlwind of emotions. This metaphor depicts lovemaking as a whirlwind of intense feelings and sensations, evoking imagery of passion and excitement.

La randonnée amoureuse: Referring to the love hike. This metaphor humorously suggests that lovemaking involves embarking on a journey of exploration and discovery, traversing the landscapes of pleasure and desire.

The Best Expressions
to Talk About Lovemaking

Jouer à touche-touche – To play touch-touch.

Visiter les catacombes - To visit the catacombs.

Monter à cheval - To ride a horse

Faire de la musique de chambre - To make bedroom music

Faire des pirouettes - To do pirouettes

Visiter les régions polaires - To visit polar regions

Faire des claquettes - To do tap dance

Faire des saltos arrière - To do back somersaults

Faire un tour de montagnes russes - To take a roller coaster ride

Monter à bord du vaisseau spatial - To board a spaceship

Faire du bricolage - To DIY (do it yourself)

Jouer à cache-cache - To play hide and seek

Monter à l'échelle - To climb the ladder

Faire de la plongée sous-marine - To go scuba diving

Se lancer dans l'exploration spatiale - To embark on space exploration

Larguer les amarres - To cast off

Se taquiner le hanneton - Teasing the cockchafer

Faire éternuer son cyclope - Make your cyclops sneeze

Branler en chocolatière - Jerking off in a chocolatier

Célébrer les pralines du samedi soir - Celebrate Saturday night pralines

Agacer le sous-préfet - Annoy the sub-prefect

Déballer le Mon Chéri - Unboxing the Mon Chéri

Planter le javelot dans la moquette - Plant the javelin in the carpet

Se désenclaver la péninsule - Opening up the peninsula

Faire une partie de traversin - Play a game of bolster

Mettre son pain au four - Put your bread in the oven

Faire des pirouettes sur le nombril - Do pirouettes on the navel

French Sayings with A Naughty or Risqué Connotation Related to Women "Cul" (Ass) and "Enculer" (to F*Ck).

*"La coquinerie, c'est l'art de taquiner
l'âme avant de séduire le corps."* — *French saying*

*(Naughtiness is the art of teasing
the soul before seducing the body.)*

When encountering the candid, often humorous descriptions used by French men when referring to women's behinds, one cannot avoid being charmed by French language and culture. From "rosette" to "wrinkled" to "with lots of mileage," French men make no secret of their fondness for directness when discussing various parts of women's bodies.

Although these remarks might appear offensive to outsiders, they demonstrate French culture's propensity to speak freely without regard for political correctness - adding charm and unfiltered honesty into daily interactions between its residents.

Avoir un cul d'enfer - **To have a hell of an ass.** Used to describe someone with an exceptionally attractive or desirable buttocks.

Le cul entre deux chaises - **The ass between two chairs.** Refers to someone who is indecisive or torn between two options.

Baiser dans le cul des vaches - **To f*ck in the ass of cows.** A vulgarity used to describe a remote or isolated location.

Avoir le cul bordé de nouilles - **To have one's ass bordered with noodles.** Used to express the feeling of being incredibly lucky or fortunate.

Se prendre une belle gamelle dans le cul - **To take a nice fall on one's ass.** Used to describe a humiliating or embarrassing failure.

La petite bête qui monte, qui monte - **The little beast that climbs, that climbs.** Humorously refers to sexual arousal or excitement, particularly in the context of foreplay.

Enculer les mouches - **To f*ck the flies.** Used to describe someone who is overly meticulous, detail-oriented or focused on trivial matters.

Les cinq à sept - The five to seven. Refers to the hours between 5 and 7 p.m., which are often associated with extramarital affairs or rendezvous with lovers.

En prendre plein le cul - To take a lot in the ass. Vulgarity used to describe someone who is facing a difficult or unpleasant situation.

Avoir un cul rebondi - To have a bouncy ass. Used to describe someone with a nicely rounded and shapely buttocks.

Avoir un cul à faire pâlir Jesus - To have an ass to make Jesus pale. Used to describe someone with an exceptionally beautiful or perfect buttocks.

Avoir un cul d'éléphant - To have an elephant's ass. Used to describe someone with a large or ample buttocks.

Mon cul sur la commode - My ass on the dresser. Humorous expression used to express disbelief or skepticism towards something.

Les pieds dans le plat et le cul entre deux chaises - Feet in the dish and ass between two chairs. Describes someone who is in an awkward or uncomfortable position, both physically and metaphorically.

S'en battre le cul par terre - To beat one's ass on the ground. Used to emphasize extreme indifference or apathy towards something.

Avoir les fesses bordées de nouilles - To have one's ass bordered with noodles. Used to express extreme luck or good fortune.

Baiser dans les chiottes - To f*ck in the toilets. Vulgarity used to describe having sex in a bathroom or restroom.

La cambrure séduisante - The seductive arch. Used to emphasize the alluring curvature of the lower back and buttocks.

Le postérieur généreux - The generous posterior. Euphemism suggesting abundance and fullness in the buttocks.

Les rondeurs charmeuses - Charming curves. Used to convey a sense of attractiveness and allure in the buttocks' shape.

Le derrière bien galbé - **The well-shaped behind**. Used to highlight the aesthetically pleasing contour and form of the buttocks.

Les fesses pulpeuses - **Plump buttocks**. Euphemism used to suggest a desirable fullness and roundness in the posterior.

Le pommeau du plumeau - **The handle of the duster**. Metaphor playfully used to liken the buttocks to the handle of a cleaning tool, emphasizing its round shape.

La pomme d'Adam - **Adam's apple**. Humorous metaphor used to compare the curvature of the buttocks to the protrusion of the throat's Adam's apple.

La lune rebelle - **The rebellious moon**. Metaphor used to evoke imagery of the moon's rounded shape, drawing a comparison to the buttocks.

La boule de billard - **The billiard ball**. Humorous metaphor used to liken the firmness and roundness of the buttocks to the smooth surface of a billiard ball.

Le coussin moelleux - **The soft cushion**. Metaphor used to compare the softness and comfort of the buttocks to a plush cushion, highlighting its inviting nature.

Un cul normal	A normal ass
Un gros cul	A big ass
Un cul mince	A slim ass
Un cul plat	A flat ass
Un cul a rosace	A rosette ass
Un cul ride	A wrinkled ass
Un cul avec beaucoup de kilometrage	An ass with lots of mileage
Un cul censuré	A censorious ass
Un cul de grande valeur	A valuable ass
Un cul tres carré	A very square ass
Un cul tres etrange	A very strange ass
Un cul cybercul	A cyber ass
Un cul mysterieux	A mysterious ass
-Un cul blessé	A hurt ass
Un cul fermé	A firm ass
Un cul a hemorroides	An ass with hemorrhoids

Breast Banter:
French Fun with Euphemisms

*"Les tétons sont les joyaux cachés du corps,
attendant d'être découverts par un aventurier intrépide!"*
— French saying

*(Nipples are the hidden jewels of the body,
waiting to be discovered by an intrepid adventurer!)*

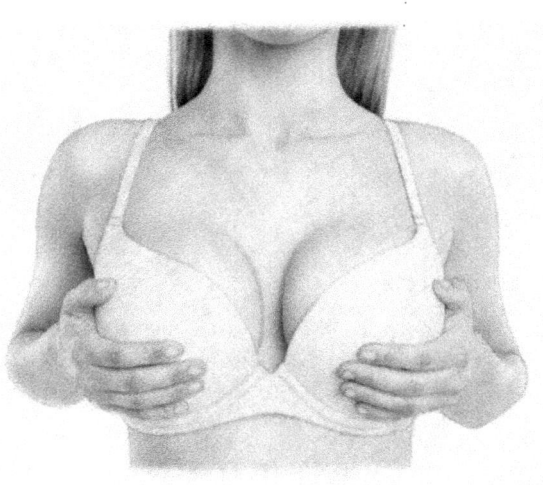

French is a language abundant with creativity; French men ingeniously employ euphemisms, each imbued with its own distinct imagery and connotation and metaphors, to playfully describe women's breasts. Enjoy!

Les atouts (The assets) - Emphasizes their value and attractiveness as a physical feature.

Les melons (The melons) - Likens their size and shape to that of melons.

Les cerises (The cherries) - Evokes their small and rounded shape, particularly when perky.

Les pastèques (The watermelons) - Highlights their large size and voluptuous nature.

Les seins (The breasts) - The most common and straightforward term.

Les tétons (The nipples) - Specifically refers to the nipples.

Les nichons (The tits) - A colloquial and slightly vulgar term.

Les lolos (The boobs) - Another informal and playful term.

Les nénés (The boobies) - A cute and affectionate term.

Les miches (The buns) - A slang term, often used humorously.

Les roploplos (The knockers) - A humorous and exaggerated term.

Les pépites (The nuggets) - A playful and endearing term.

Les doudounes (The puffy ones) - A cute and affectionate term, often used in a playful context.

Les ballons (The balloons) - Evokes their round shape, particularly when they are large.

Les bosquets (The groves) - Suggests their soft and rounded appearance.

Les pommes (The apples) - Refers to their shape, particularly when they are perky.

Les charmes (The charms) - Implies their allure and attractiveness.

Les joyeux lurons (The merry ones) - Playful and jovial term suggesting a sense of fun and liveliness.

Les douceurs (The sweet ones) - Evokes their softness and tenderness.

Les galbes (The contours) - Highlights their shapeliness and elegance.

Les fraises (The strawberries) - Implies their small and delicate appearance, akin to strawberries.

Les raisins (The grapes) - Likens their clustered appearance to a bunch of grapes.

Les prunes (The plums) – Hints at their rounded and slightly elongated shape.

Les abricots (The apricots) - Evokes their small and rounded appearance, akin to apricots.

Les citrons (The lemons) - Highlights their small and perky nature, akin to lemons.

Les bouées (The buoys) - Suggests their buoyancy and the support they provide.

Les bimbelotiers (The bauble holders) - Evokes the idea of them as holders of decorative trinkets.

Les bosselés (The dented ones) - A humorous term, implying their natural contours and imperfections.

Les délices (The delights) - Highlights their pleasure and sensuality.

Les amandes (The almonds) - Likens their shape to that of almonds, particularly when perky.

Les balluchons (The bundles) - Implies their rounded and bundled appearance.

Les toisons (The fleeces) - Suggests their soft and fuzzy texture.

Les pendules (The pendulums) - Refers to those that sway or swing with movement.

Les réservoirs (The reservoirs) - Likens them to storage tanks, suggesting abundance and fullness.

Les calebasses (The gourds) – Compares them to round and full shape of the breasts with the fruit.

Les obus (The shells) - Evokes a sense of power and impact, often used to describe larger breasts.

Les p'tits pains (The little loaves) - A cute and affectionate term comparing them to small bread rolls.

Les pralines (The pralines) - Implies their sweetness and delicacy.

Les globes (The globes) - Highlights their rounded and spherical shape.

Les pilons (The drumsticks) - A playful comparison, suggesting their tapered shape.

Les pendouilles (The danglers) - Refers to ones that are more pendulous or droopy.

Les flotteurs (The floaters) - Suggests their buoyant and weightless quality.

Les coussinets (The cushions) - Evokes a sense of softness and comfort, likening them to cushions.

Les gaufres (The waffles) - A humorous comparison, highlighting their textured appearance.

From Rising to Happy Endings:
The Tale of Male Sexual Shenanigans!

Il n'existe pratiquement aucune différence entre un Anglais en erection et un Italien impuissant. — Frédéric Dard

(There is practically no difference between an erect Englishman and an impotent Italian.)

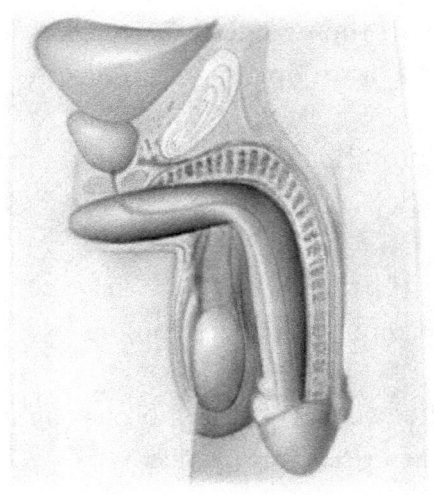

Male sexual responses involve an intricate series of physiological processes that culminate in erection and ejaculation:

Stimulation and Arousal

Stimulation typically begins the sexual response cycle. Physical, visual, auditory or psychological stimuli, such as physical contact, can all act to release neurotransmitters, such as dopamine, which trigger the brain's reward system and increase arousal levels.

Erection

When arousal increases, the brain sends signals to the penis's arteries to dilate and increase blood flow to erectile tissues, leading to swelling and erection. An increase in blood flow causes corpora cavernosa chambers inside the penis to fill with blood and expand, leading to firm erections; at the same time, veins that normally drain blood contract to maintain and ensure an erection's long-term success.

Plateau Phase

Once erect, the penis transitions into a plateau phase, marked by sustained arousal. The penis remains erect and highly responsive to stimulation, resulting in enhanced sexual pleasure.

Ejaculation

When sexual stimulation continues, the body prepares for ejaculation by contracting pelvic floor muscles, including the bulbocavernosus and ischiocavernosus muscles, located in the pelvic floor area. -that will push semen from the seminal vesicle and prostate gland into the urethra for formation; simultaneously, the bladder neck closes to prevent urine mixing with semen. Then, rhythmic contractions between muscles located on pelvic floor/base of penis force semen out in series of ejaculatory spurts.

Resolution and Refractory Period

After ejaculation, the body enters a resolution phase, during which arousal gradually subsides and the penis returns to its flaccid state. A refractory period follows this, where it becomes difficult or impossible for individuals to elicit another erection and orgasm; the duration varies among individuals but generally increases with age.

At every point in this process, a variety of hormones, neurotransmitters and physiological mechanisms, including health, stress levels, medications and relationship dynamics, interact to produce male sexual responses.

Bedroom Aerobics:
How Getting Busy Boosts Bro Health and Happiness!

"Faire l'amour, c'est comme créer une œuvre d'art érotique, où chaque caresse est un coup de pinceau sur la toile de la sensualité!" — French citation

(Making love is like creating an erotic work of art, where each caress is a brushstroke on the canvas of sensuality!)

Engaging in regular sexual activity has many health and wellbeing advantages for men:

Physical Health

Regular sexual activity can improve cardiovascular health by increasing blood circulation and decreasing risk factors associated with heart disease.

Strengthens the Immune System

Due to increased production of antibodies and strengthened defense mechanisms, sexual activity may boost men's immune systems.

Eases Pain

Sexual activity releases endorphins that act as natural painkillers that may help relieve headaches, and other forms of discomfort.

Improves Sleep

Orgasm stimulates the release of hormones, such as oxytocin and prolactin, that aid relaxation, leading to improved sleep quality.

Mental and Emotional Well-Being

Sexual activity promotes endorphin release, lowers cortisol levels and can act as an effective, natural stress reliever.

Improves Mood

By creating feelings of intimacy, connection, and pleasure, regular sex can help to elevate mood and alleviate symptoms of depression and anxiety.

Enhances Self-Esteem

Engaging in positive sexual experiences can contribute to enhanced feelings of self-worth and confidence.

Increases Relationship Satisfaction

For those in committed relationships, sexual activity can play an invaluable role in building emotional intimacy and strengthening bonds between partners.

Prostate Health

According to recent research, sexual activity or masturbation that promotes ejaculation could help lower the risk of prostate cancer by flushing out potentially dangerous substances from within the gland.

Hormonal Balance

Sexual activity can help maintain balanced hormonal levels, especially testosterone, which plays an essential role in muscle mass, bone density and libido development.

Studies have identified correlations between sexual activity and increased longevity, suggesting that leading a healthy sexual life may extend lifespan.

While more sexual encounters may offer potential advantages, the quality of experiences (as well as overall health and well-being) play an equally vital role. Communication, mutual consent and a positive approach toward sexuality are integral parts of experiencing an enjoyable sexual life.

Unveiling Comedy: Growers vs Show-ers

What should we keep in mind regarding penis growers versus show-ers?

You have likely observed that the size of the penis at rest depends on various external and internal factors that impact its true size, such as stress, fear, anxiety, and temperature changes.

Many men think that the size of their penis when not erect shows how big it will be when it is erect; so, they assume there's a connection between the size of a hard penis and a soft one.

But that's not true! As we talked about earlier, it depends on how many spaces are inside a penis to hold blood, which could mean more growth than in a bigger penis when it's not erected.

No matter their penis type - whether grower or show-er - all men can experience erectile dysfunction. Rest assured: there's no predisposition to male impotence. If you have trouble getting an erection, do not hesitate to visit a physician who may suggest appropriate treatment and/or possibly recommend Viagra or Cialis.

Premature ejaculation equally affects all types of penises. If it becomes an issue for you, don't try self-medicating - consult a healthcare provider.

Does size matter?

It depends; just as penises are different, so are women's bodies, and some women need larger penises to feel satisfied.

There's no point in suffering from complexes. We don't hear better if we have big ears. This can apply to the penis. Better a small, vigorous penis than a big, lazy one.

Unmasking Men's Misadventures: Sex, Lies and Shrinking Cocks

"Pour les hommes, les femmes sont comme des énigmes qui donnent un sens à leur existence." — Julien

(For men, women are like puzzles that give meaning to their existence.)

How long should sexual intercourse last?

Ah, the ideal length of a love-making session! In France, we treat lovemaking like fine wine: every sip should be an enjoyable journey! Some prefer an espresso, while others enjoy an indulging cafe au lait – usually, it takes 5 to 7 minutes before magic occurs! Ultimately, though, enjoy yourself without being preoccupied by time! When it comes to pleasure, quality trumps quantity! So, let yourself be carried away by passion without looking at the clock! Cheers and happy tasting!

Does a woman need sex every day to become pregnant?

Conceiving a baby can be an intricate process. Some may mistakenly believe frequent intimacy is essential; in reality, conception depends on timing within a woman's cycle rather than regular intimacy. My advice? Don't put too much emphasis on regular intimacy - embrace romantic moments at your own rhythm and trust nature's timing to take its course; spontaneity adds much-needed depth and richness to lovemaking experience.

Do sexual positions promote conception?

No scientific evidence exists to back this assertion. While some swear by certain exercises to increase fertility, Mother Nature ultimately controls her own rhythm - sometimes the simplest moves can be the most successful! Therefore, whether dancing the tango or the cha-cha, remember it's not about steps but chemistry between partners that matters when it comes to love and conception.

Does penis size matter when it comes to getting pregnant?

Gentlemen... it's not the size of the boat, it's the motion of the ocean! When it comes to conception, success lies not with grand vessels, but in how sailors navigate the waters. Do not fret over dimensions; instead, prioritize passion with finesse and skill! Success is, ultimately, determined by its captain.

Should sexuality and religion be kept separate?

It's a lively debate! We have a saying in French: "Chacun son goût!" i.e., "To each their own taste!" You see, when it comes to matters of the heart and the divine, everyone has his/her own recipe for happiness. Some may find harmony in the union of spirituality and sensuality, while others prefer to keep their prayers and pleasures separate. But, hey - if you're spreading love and joy, whether in the chapel or the bedroom, who am I to judge? After all, life is like a fine Bordeaux – it's all about finding the perfect blend that tickles your taste buds! Cheers to love, laughter and the pursuit of happiness, gentlemen!

How to care for our beloved member?

In France, manhood is treated with the same reverence as a fine Champagne – with great care and attention to detail. When it comes to essential penis care, it's all about pampering and protection. Just like a prized vintage, our penis deserves the royal treatment!

First and foremost, cleanliness is key! A daily rinse with warm water and a gentle cleanser will keep things fresh and inviting. Think of it as giving your prized possession a luxurious bubble bath!

Next, don't forget the moisturizer! Just like a fine wine needs its cork, our penis needs its hA dab of moisturizer, preferably one with natural ingredients, keeps our manhood soft, supple and ready for action.

And let's not overlook protection! Much like a sommelier protects their finest bottle, we must safeguard our member with the proper attire. That means always using protection during intimate encounters to keep our prized possession safe and sound.

So, my fellow connoisseurs of the male anatomy, remember to treat your penis with the love and care it deserves.

After all, it's not just a body part – it's a work of art! Cheers to happy and healthy manhood, gentlemen!

What is the foreskin used for? Can it be removed as an adult?

It serves to preserve the sensitivity of the glans. Yes, it can be removed as an adult. It's called circumcision, and its benefit is the reduction in the risk of genital infections.

Can the length of the same man's erect penis vary from one day to the next?

Manhood is like the Eiffel Tower: sometimes standing tall and proud, other times taking a restful siesta. But don't panic - just like Paris weather conditions can change rapidly over time, so, too, can a penis's length vary daily!

Penises are fickle creatures, often surprising us with unpredictable but captivating behavior. On any given day, it might reach for the stars; on another, it might choose a low-profile approach - just like trying to predict a French romance! It is truly captivating!

So, my fellow gentlemen, don't fret if your manhood decides to take a day off or stand at attention like a soldier on parade. Embrace its quirks and fluctuations and remember that variety is the spice of life! After all, in matters of love and anatomy, it's the joie de vivre that truly counts!

Is penis length important for penetration?

Penetration isn't about using a big sword like a musketeer; it's about knowing how to use it smoothly and skillfully.

Think of pastry baking like playing a cornhole game precision and technique are of utmost importance! So, whether it's baguettes or croissants you're working with, don't get distracted by size; what truly impresses is the artistry of the baker.

Let's not overlook passion and connection! Ultimately, what matters is not how long the journey is; rather, it is the enjoyment of each step that matters the most! So, men, embrace all you've been given, and remember when it comes to love and loaves, it's the quality, not quantity, that leaves a lasting impression! Live the love!

However, it is not always true for every woman. Some may prefer thickness over length. And it's not just about moving back and forth; it's more about rocking with your hips when you're erect. So, instead of worrying about size, focus on improving your hip movements.

What is the difference between a circumcised penis and an uncircumcised penis?

Dear friends, welcome to the age-old debate between circumcised and uncircumcised individuals! In France, it can be likened to the difference between comparing baguettes and croissants - each delicious in their own ways yet have distinct characteristics!

As previously discussed, the main difference lies in the presence of foreskin. With a circumcised penis, its foreskin is removed to create an elegant and streamlined appearance, reminiscent of newly pruned vineyards; on the other hand, an uncircumcised penis retains its natural covering, resembling delicate flower buds waiting to bloom.

How they operate during sexual activity, however, is ultimately up to individual preference and technique! Some may argue that circumcising provides a smoother ride, like sailing on the Seine on a quiet summer's day, while, for others, an uncircumcised penis offers more of an immersive experience, like traversing Montmartre's cobblestone streets.

But fear not, my fellow men - no matter your circumcision status, it's all about finding what works best for you and your partner. At the core of it all lies the connection and chemistry that drives love relationships forward! Here's to celebrating our differences! Vive la différence.

Curved penis: is there any solution (other than surgery) to straighten it?

Are you tired of crooked baguettes? Don't worry, the French saying, "There is more than one way to bend one," means that there are multiple methods of shaping a baguette.

Indeed, surgery may be an option for some individuals; however, other avenues should first be explored before turning to surgical solutions. Exercise and techniques can help gently straighten and strengthen your member like clay when molding.

Seeking advice from medical professionals or licensed therapists may provide invaluable insight and direction on how best to address your unique circumstances. In matters relating to health and happiness, it's vitally important to explore all possible avenues before making a final decision.

So, don't give up hope! With some patience and persistence, even the crookedest baguettes can prove rewarding.

Do you happen to own an overly large loaf?

I have had a large and thick penis since adolescence, which bothers me in daily life. Can it be reduced?

Have no fear! Solutions exist that could help to reduce its dimensions. While decreasing its dimensions might not be easy, there are methods and treatments you could try that could work wonders; who knows? You might even discover people willing to trade places with you! Consulting medical experts or specialized therapists could offer valuable strategies tailored specifically to you and your situation.

Is it concerning not to experience nocturnal or morning erections?

Yes and no. As we age, morning erections tend to become less frequent, as testosterone levels fluctuate and affect erectile function. Don't panic - while their absence may raise some eyebrows, it often shouldn't cause alarm.

At first, this may be worrying; but keep in mind that our bodies have their own rhythms, and any fluctuations are part of life's journey.

However, if you notice other worrying changes, it's always advisable to consult a medical professional, as they can offer valuable reassurance and guidance tailored specifically for you. Therefore, gentlemen, when it comes to health and happiness, it is always better to err on the side of caution.

Are changes to penis hardness normal as we age?

Absolutely. Studies indicate that 15-20% of men aged 50 may experience a decline in erection strength. But don't despair - in France, we believe age is nothing but a number, and our baguettes will still rise to meet any challenge!

Though things will naturally soften over time, proper care and attention can help maintain satisfactory firmness. Regular exercise, healthy nutrition and reduced stress are the keys to keeping your baguette at its peak - it thrives with love!

Don't let age dampen your spirits! With some TLC, your baguette can continue to impress!

How We Can Navigate the Pitfalls of Porn: A French Perspective

French society understands the allure and risks of pornography. Excessive consumption may alter perceptions of intimacy and lead to unrealistic expectations, desensitizing individuals and inducing negative emotions (in much the same way as extreme alcohol use does). Moderation is key for maintaining mental and emotional well-being.

Can those who identify as asexual, can one undergo a surgical procedure to remove the penis?

Penis removal may not always be necessary; if it is not actively used, removal may not be required. But prior to considering such an approach, medical advice must always be sought and understood fully; researching asexuality's implications for identity and relationships will provide further insight. Ultimately, any decision must be made with care and honesty in mind.

What is a hermaphrodite?

Hermaphrodites are individuals whose genes make them part man and part woman, producing estrogen and testosterone in different proportions at any one time. There is no defined sexual identity. Due to outdated and stigmatizing connotations of the term "hermaphrodite," modern medical and scientific contexts tend to prefer "intersex," which recognizes differences between sexual characteristics that transcend typical male/female categories.

Is there a correlation between the size of feet, hands, and nose with penis size?

Scientific evidence does not support a correlation between feet size, hands size or nose size with penis size; each physical trait is determined by different genetic factors that differ among individuals and vary independently over time. Therefore, making assumptions based solely on physical traits as the only predictors for penis size would be inaccurate.

Does sex = penetration?

Although penetration is an integral aspect of sexual activity, restricting its definition solely to this act would miss the point. Sexuality entails many activities, beyond penetration, that can bring pleasure and intimacy; its definition varies among individuals and cultures alike. Recognizing and respecting diversity among sexual preferences and practices, as well as understanding that intimacy may manifest itself through various avenues beyond just penetration, is crucial for an enriching sexual life experience.

So...no. Penetration is just one option of making love; there are various methods.

Is it normal for the penis to have a distinct odor?

Yes, it's normal due to sweat and bacteria. Maintaining good hygiene, including regular washing with mild soap, can help reduce any lingering smells. If the odor persists or becomes particularly strong, it's advisable to consult a healthcare professional to rule out any underlying issues.

Does the foreskin facilitate masturbation?

Yes of course! The foreskin makes it easier to slide. Without a foreskin, we tend to use lubricants.

Does a man only experience erection when aroused?

No - an erection occurs whenever a man becomes aroused due to his brain processes - I experience them both during the day and at night! Although I can't speak for all men on Earth, I can tell you one thing - an erection can happen in response to physical stimulation or subconscious factors during sleep. This natural physiological reaction differs according to everyone.

Does a penis count as muscle?

No; instead, it consists of soft spongy tissue and blood vessels that fill with blood to produce an erection. While not technically considered muscle tissue (like that found in skeletal muscles), there are certain muscle components within its makeup, such as bulbospongiosus and ischiocavernosus muscles, which help control erections and ejaculation, respectively.

More Facts About Penises

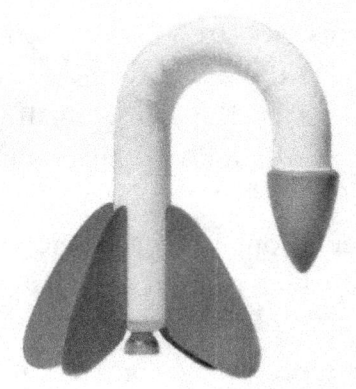

This amazing tool for reproduction and pleasure still holds many mysteries:

1. A museum dedicated to the penis is in Reykjavik, Iceland. There are 217 different penises there, all species combined.

2. The penis is a nest of bacteria. There are 42 types of bacteria found only on the penis. A circumcised penis has fewer.

3. Penis size does not matter when conceiving a child.

4. The male penis measures on average 9 cm at rest and 14 cm when erect. The world record for the longest penis is held by the American actor Jonah Falcon. His penis is 9.5 inches at rest and 13.5 inches when erect.

5. During ejaculation, the penis ejects 3 milliliters of sperm, or 20 to 150 million sperm.

6. The penis is erect, on average, 11 times a day and nine times during the night.

7. 45 km/hour is the peak speed of sperm at the time of ejaculation.

8. The smallest penis in the world is 1.6 cm; the man in question prefers to remain anonymous. He's somewhere in the state of Mississippi.

9. Because nicotine, the chemical substance in tobacco, affects blood circulation, smoking alters erections and causes erectile disorders.

10. The penis can fracture even though it is not physically a bone.

11. Avoid abstinence; in the absence of sexual relations, the penis can lose between 1 and 2 cm.

12. Six seconds is the average duration of the male orgasm.

13. A male fetus begins its erections in its mother's womb.

14. Straight penises are rare.

15- In Australia, the males of the Walibri tribe do not use their hands to greet others – grabbing genitals is the way to say hello!

Bedtime Blunders:
Mistakes Every Man Should Avoid and Tips from a French Flirt

"Le secret pour être un bon amant réside dans la passion de donner du plaisir, pas seulement d'en recevoir." — *Pascal*

(The secret to being a good lover lies in the passion for giving pleasure, not just receiving it.)

1. Do not call your partner the name of an ex.

2. Hygiene might seem elementary, but you must still try to ensure its upkeep.

3. Never attempt to penetrate a woman without first applying lubricant.

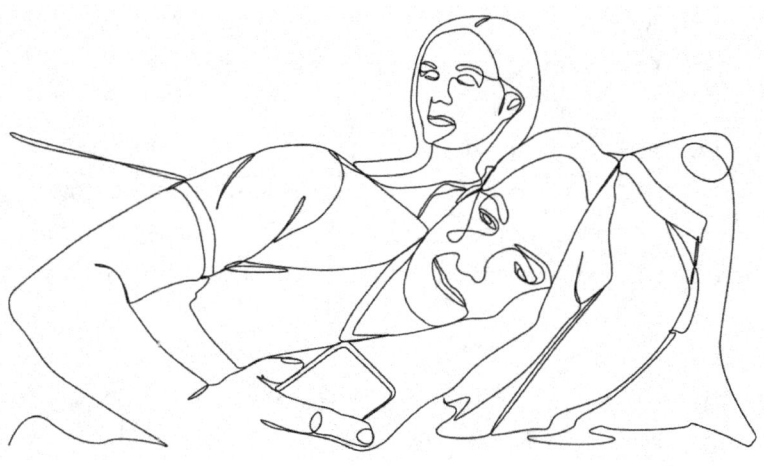

4. Don't overlook kissing; it is vitally important! Hypocretins sensors stimulate sexual arousal, producing pleasure and orgasm in response to kissing, creating more opportunities to bond and feel closer.

5. Choose an unconventional sexual method. As everyone's needs vary, what works for Kimberly may not necessarily apply to Summer; making this mistake would be disastrous!

6. Not everyone enjoys dirty talk during sexual encounters; sometimes, sweeter words may be more appropriate. Take the time to understand your partner - what

she does and doesn't like, as well as her expectations - before engaging in a sexual encounter.

7. Do not give any inaccurate feedback to your partner. Pretending that everything is alright when it may not be is not recommended; communication must be ongoing to determine what works and what doesn't in the bedroom.

8. Being negative and speaking toxically to your partner during or prior to a sexual encounter are behaviors to avoid.

9. We can still enjoy closeness without needing to have sex. Many men overlook the pleasures of things like kissing, touching, and caressing other parts of the body besides penetration.

10. Don't reach for your phone after engaging in a sexual activity (an enormous faux pas). Sex doesn't end just because the act has concluded!

11. Immediately vacating the bed after enjoying your indulgence is an act of extreme self-interest.

12. Skipping straight to intercourse without sufficient foreplay is not ideal. It's important to make time for foreplay, including activities like kissing, touching, and oral stimulation, to enhance arousal and pleasure for both partners.

13. Communication is imperative between partners to ensure mutual satisfaction. Discuss preferences, desires, boundaries, and fantasies openly to maximize success. Assuming without asking or failing to express desires and preferences can lead to misunderstandings.

14. Focusing solely on penetration is not the only way to please a partner.

15. To provide diverse sources of pleasure, explore various sexual activities, such as oral sex, manual stimulation, and sensual massage.

16. Do not rush to climax!

17. Take your time and focus on enjoying every step along your journey of sexual intimacy without being in a rush to reach the finish line. Savor each moment and sensation as they come without pushing too hard towards reaching that destination.

18. Failing to prioritize clitoral stimulation during sex is common. Remember that many women require clitoral stimulation to achieve orgasm, so it's important to incorporate manual or oral stimulation of the clitoris into your sexual repertoire.

19. Focusing solely on yourself without considering your partner's needs or desires is a faux pas. Practice reciprocity in the bedroom by prioritizing your partner's pleasure and satisfaction as much as your own.

20. Pay attention to nonverbal cues during sexual encounters. Failing to acknowledge or interpret them can be seen as disrespectful. Be attentive to your partner's body language, facial expressions, and vocalizations to gauge their level of interest or excitement.

21. Neglecting emotional intimacy during sexual encounters is a mistake. Building emotional intimacy with your partner, both inside and outside the bedroom, fosters trust, communication, and affection.

22. Prioritize personal hygiene during sexual encounters. Shower regularly, trim pubic hair, and use protection to prevent the spread of infections.

23. Avoid criticizing or being overly self-conscious about your body or performance. Embrace self-acceptance and body positivity, focusing on pleasure, connection, and enjoyment rather than perfection or performance.

24. Ensure mutual pleasure by being gentle and attentive during sexual activities, avoiding excessive pressure. Gradually adjust pressure and communicate with your partner to respect their comfort and boundaries.

25. Recognize the importance of lubrication during sexual encounters. Natural lubrication may not be sufficient for comfort.

26. Utilize water-based or silicone-based lubricants as needed to enhance comfort and reduce friction, particularly if vaginal dryness is a concern.

27. Prioritize safe sex practices to prevent the transmission of sexually transmitted diseases (STDs) and unwanted pregnancies. Consistently and correctly use condoms to ensure protection.

28. Avoid sticking to the same routine or sexual positions every time—lack of variety can be a mistake. Explore new sexual positions, fantasies, role-playing scenarios,

and erotic activities to keep things exciting and fresh in the bedroom.

29. Do not underestimate the importance of aftercare—neglecting emotional and physical aftercare following sexual activity can be a mistake. Practice aftercare by cuddling, talking, and showing affection afterward, providing emotional support and reassurance for your partner.

30. Maintain focus during sexual intimacy and avoid distractions such as phones, TV, or work-related stress. Create a distraction-free environment that allows both partners to stay present during sexual encounters, free from interruption from devices and other sources of noise or disruptions.

31. Avoid placing undue pressure on yourself to perform or achieve specific outcomes. Instead, prioritize pleasure, connection, and mutual enjoyment with your partner, moving away from performance goals.

32. Disregarding consent is a mistake. Always obtain clear and enthusiastic consent from your partner before engaging in sexual activity, always respecting boundaries and preferences.

33. Avoid comparing your partner's physical appearance or sexual performance to others. Instead, focus on acknowledging your partner's uniqueness and appreciating their individual qualities, fostering intimacy and connection between two people.

34. Prioritize sexual health by scheduling regular STD screenings, discussing sexual health concerns openly with your partner, and practicing safer sex. Avoid neglecting regular sexual health check-ups or avoiding discussions about sexual health.

35. Remain open-minded and receptive to constructive feedback from your partner, using it as an opportunity to improve communication and enhance sexual experiences together. Avoid disregarding or reacting defensively to feedback or suggestions from your partner.

36. Recognize that sexual satisfaction is multifaceted and can involve various aspects of intimacy, pleasure, and emotional connection beyond achieving orgasm. Orgasm is not the sole measure of sexual satisfaction or success.

37. Practice relaxation techniques, such as deep breathing or mindfulness, to manage performance anxiety and focus on the present moment with your partner. Avoid allowing performance anxiety or pressure to negatively impact sexual experiences.

38. Embrace the diversity of sexual experiences and recognize that simultaneous orgasm is not necessary for mutual satisfaction. Instead, focus on pleasure, connection, and intimacy. Avoid expecting simultaneous orgasm for sex to be fulfilling.

39. Remember, after sexual activity, it's crucial not to overlook aftercare. Prioritize both your emotional and physical needs. Engage in activities that foster relaxation, self-reflection, and emotional well-being. Take ample time to process your experiences and show yourself compassion. Your self-care matters.

The 40 Stupidest Sex Myths Many Men Believe: Let's Restore The Truth and Stop These False Beliefs!

"Les mythes sont les étoiles qui guident notre imagination à travers les ténèbres de l'inconnu." — LoLo

(Myths are the stars that guide our imagination through the darkness of the unknown.)

1. Green M&Ms are an aphrodisiac.

2. The size of a man's penis is proportional to the size of his feet.

3. Masturbation makes you deaf or blind.

4. The average size of a penis is 20 cm.

5. Circumcised men have better erections.

6. Men think about sex every seven seconds; in fact, only 23% of males think about it at this frequency.

7. Women are incapable of making love without feelings; more and more are enjoying "one-night stands."

8. It is possible to break a penis. It is more of a tear of the corpus cavernosum than a classic fracture.

9. Men enjoy sex more than women.

10. Sex should last two hours. (The average duration of sexual intercourse is between three and seven minutes.)

11. Men with big noses have big penises.

12. The more beautiful you are, the better you make love.

13. Making love drunk or high increases prowess.

14. Pornography provides ideas for better love making.

15. You can catch an STD in public toilets.

16. Swingers are happier.

17. Making love with a condom is not really making love.

18. The condoms distributed by the government are of poor quality.

19. Condoms make you sick.

20. Men poke holes in condoms.

21. If men don't have sex or masturbate, they may suffer from sperm blockage.

22. Heat makes a man impotent.

23. No erection, no arousal. The absence of an erection is often considered a sign of lack of desire.

24. Men have a G-spot. A prostate is not a G spot.

25. A condom makes you last longer in bed.

26. A condom reduces performance in bed.

27. People of color have bigger appendages.

28. A vaginal orgasm is associated with better sexual satisfaction in women.

29. Menstruation is dirty.

30. Elevating your wife's legs and hips after sex increases the chances of getting pregnant.

31. Penis size matters, and bigger is always better.

32. There are magic pills or supplements that can instantly enhance sexual stamina and performance.

33. Both partners should achieve simultaneous orgasms every time, like clockwork.

34. Sexual prowess and techniques seen in pornography translate to real-life sexual encounters.

35. Having one signature move or technique is enough to satisfy a partner in bed.

36. Talking about sexual desires, preferences or concerns with a partner is unnecessary or taboo.

37. Wearing a condom significantly reduces pleasure for both partners, leading to avoiding condom use altogether.

38. Masturbation is always superior to partnered sex and can replace the need for intimacy.

39. Every woman has a hidden "magic button" or G-spot hat, when found, guarantees orgasm every time.

40. Sexual performance is solely based on physical techniques and not on emotional connection, communication and mutual pleasure.

Essentials:
Sleeping Naked Together - Examining Its Intimate Advantages for Couples!

*"Dormir nu avec quelqu'un est l'intimité ultime,
une vulnérabilité partagée sous les draps." — GB*

*(Sleeping naked with someone is the ultimate intimacy,
a shared vulnerability beneath the sheets.)*

Sleeping naked together should never be forced upon either partner in a relationship, yet its benefits should still be acknowledged by both.

1. Sleeping naked together makes you yearn to make love more.

2. Direct skin-to-skin contact triggers the production of Oxytocin, an attachment hormone.

3. Communication in relationships should go beyond verbal exchanges - touch is also an important form of expression.

4. Sleeping naked may help your partner gain more self-assurance and, over time, feel freer, more fulfilled and less self-conscious.

5. Sleeping naked is natural and encourages blood circulation.

Spice Up Your Bedroom Menu: Exploring the French Art of Intimate Variety

"La variété est la source de tout plaisir."
— Madame de Sévigné

(Variety is the source of all pleasure.)

Just as eating the same dish every day can become monotonous, so can maintaining the same sexual positions night after night. Explore new avenues of intimacy to stay passionate and romantic in relationships. To keep things fresh and the spark ignited, it's essential that you explore all options available!

Contrary to popular belief, there's no hard and fast rule regarding how often couples should make love; instead, couples should find an optimal rhythm that works best for both. Pornography may give an inkling into these acrobatic positions; however, these depictions often fall far short of reality and may even present risks, such as penile fractures.

As part of an effort to add some variety into bedroom adventures, a French magazine conducted a poll among women living in France to discover their top three favorite sexual positions. Not only did these positions provide exciting variations, but they also allowed participants to break away from sexual routines and explore alternative positions.

Missionary: Hailed as the iconic position, this position offers couples the chance to experience deeper connection and intimacy than any other. Allowing for face-to-face contact while maintaining eye contact, this posture offers emotional closeness as well as passionate encounters. (include illustrative photos)

Doggy Style: For an exciting and thrilling bedroom escapade, doggy style can add a new element of penetration and dominance to your escapades. Allowing deeper penetration while giving each partner ample opportunity to further explore one another's bodies. (include illustrations as needed)

Spooning: Clasping hands when spooning creates intimacy while providing relaxation and comfort. Spooning not only offers an intimate moment but also fosters a tender connection between partners, providing a sense of security and intimacy. It serves as an intimate gesture that strengthens the bond and enhances the closeness between partners.

Implementing these positions into your sexual repertoire can help reduce monotony and restore passion in your relationship. Remember, successful intimacy lies in open communication, mutual exploration and the willingness to embrace new experiences together.

Sexual Activity, Household Conflicts and Rumors Among Men: Is There Any Danger in this Mix?

*"La rumeur est comme une boule de neige,
plus on la fait rouler, plus elle grossit."*
— French saying

*(Rumor is like a snowball - the more you roll it,
the bigger it gets.)*

Recently, I had an interesting discussion with a former work colleague. He mentioned studies conducted in the United States revealing that men who actively take part in household chores may experience less sexual activity compared to those who don't - it almost seems as though their masculinity gets lost amongst all that dishwashing liquid!

As noted by this author, men who engage in traditionally masculine activities tend to experience more frequent sexual encounters. Could household chores be secretly undermining our love lives? Who wants to risk losing their manhood due to a sink full of dishes?

I asked him to share his sources with me. I am still waiting.

Therefore, my fellow gentlemen, it may be beneficial to delegate "feminine" tasks, such as housework, to your partner to preserve your virility. Instead, try engaging in activities like gardening or working on the car to maintain masculine energy - as a ride on the vacuum cleaner likely won't lead to romance!

He also shared four phrases you should never say to your wife (unless she is sick or pregnant):

1. "Don't worry, I'll take care of the cleaning, Darling. It's my turn to vacuum."

2. "What would you like for dinner tonight? I can arrange that."

3. "Trust in me, Dear; I'll do the dishes."

While there might be stories or cultural ideas linking men who do household chores with their sex lives, it's important to approach these claims carefully. Studies examining this correlation exist; it's crucial that one carefully evaluates its methodology and findings before drawing any definitive conclusions about whether these claims hold water. It should also be noted that some claims may simply be perpetuated rumors by societal stereotypes. My perspective is that both partners need to contribute toward fulfilling household responsibilities within relationships - something I am still laughing over!

Transatlantic Dating Insights: Wisdom from a Frenchman for American Men

"L'homme et la femme sont comme les deux faces d'une médaille: complémentaires et indispensables l'un à l'autre."
— Simone de Beauvoir

(Man and woman are like the two sides of a coin: complementary and indispensable to each other.)

#1 Women are often drawn to men who set ambitious goals and pursue their passions with enthusiasm, as these qualities tend to make them more attractive.

#2 Personal growth, crucial for maintaining attractiveness, may be overlooked. A man who sets and pursues challenging goals, aligned with his passions, is likely to be consistently appealing to women.

#3 As the feminist movement gained traction, I embraced independent thinking. While I value many of feminists' arguments, I choose not to unquestioningly adopt their viewpoints but, rather, to appreciate them in moderation.

Without adopting an overly masculine stance, I believe it's important for men not to center their lives around women or any single woman.

True attractiveness stems from achieving personal goals, not from living solely to please women or becoming subservient to them. Your pursuits should be driven by your own passions, not solely focused on pleasing others. Appreciate women, but prioritize living for yourself; men who captivate women are those with compelling lives centered around their own aspirations and interests.

#4 Non communication stands out as a primary factor contributing to divorce. Despite women typically uttering about 20,000 more words per day than the average man (approximately 13,000 more!), effective communication—particularly tailored to women's needs—remains a challenge. Merely talking more doesn't equate to superior communication skills.

Throughout my dating experiences, I have discovered the importance of refraining from attempting to solve women's problems; these are their challenges to navigate. Instead, maintaining a calm demeanor proves most effective—especially when interacting with French women (a principle that can, perhaps, also apply to American women).

I also learned to decipher the language of American women:

• "Yes" often means "no"

• "No" unequivocally means "no"

• "Maybe" essentially means "no"

• "Do what you wish" essentially means "no"

#5 For men, carving out time for themselves and their friends is essential for cultivating happiness. This doesn't diminish the enjoyment of being with their significant other; rather, it acknowledges the value of occasional solitude and male bonding.

#6 My cousin, navigating a challenging divorce, confided in me his enduring love for his wife, despite their separation. He admitted to often accepting fault to maintain peace, but this approach ultimately deteriorated their relationship.

Believing that women favor niceness is misguided. Yielding to avoid conflict or consistently agreeing with them leads to long-term failure. Being polite to women doesn't guarantee sexual favors, unlike with men. Surrendering dignity may bring women closer, but men's sexual needs are equally valid. Inappropriate discussions or fantasies won't win favor; respect is key.

Kindness is admirable, but it shouldn't be confused with weakness.

Conclusion

"Le désir sexuel, c'est comme une tempête:
parfois dévastateur, mais toujours électrisant."
— French saying

(Translation: sexual desire is like a storm:
sometimes devastating, but always electrifying.)

The humorous nicknames that French men use for their
penises, often through euphemisms and metaphors, reflect
not only a playful aspect of their culture, but also an
appreciation for linguistic creativity. From endearing
terms like "le petit Jesus" (the little Jesus) to more imagi-
native monikers, such as "la baguette magique" (the magic
wand), these nicknames showcase the French penchant for
wit and charm, even in the most intimate aspects of life.
For Francophiles and non-French speakers alike, exploring
these linguistic gems can offer a delightful glimpse into
the rich tapestry of French culture and language. More-

over, embracing the lightheartedness and creativity inherent in these nicknames can serve as a reminder to cherish and enjoy the gift of masculinity. Rather than viewing the topic with embarrassment or taboo, finding inspiration in the French approach can foster a healthier and more positive attitude towards one's own manhood. After all, language has the power to transform the mundane into objects of fascination and joy, and the French language exemplifies this beautifully when it comes to celebrating the human body and its quirks. So, whether one is a Francophile or simply curious about linguistic playfulness, exploring the world of French euphemisms for the male anatomy can be both entertaining and enlightening.